CLOTHES AND CRAFTS IN HISTORY

CLOTHES AND CRAFTS IN
AZTEC TIMES

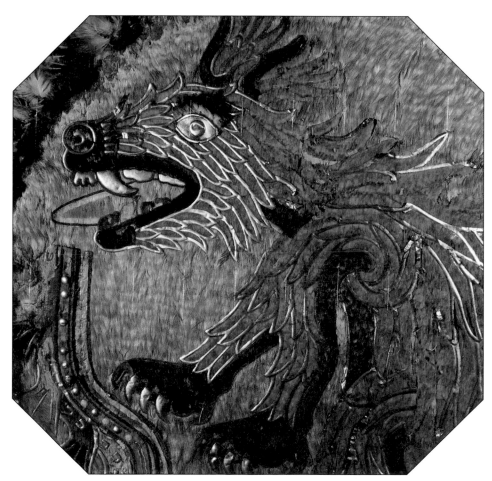

Imogen Dawson

Gareth Stevens Publishing
A WORLD ALMANAC EDUCATION GROUP COMPANY

Gareth Stevens Publishing would like to thank Lance R. Grahn, Ph.D., Associate Professor of History, Marquette University, Milwaukee, Wisconsin, for his kind and professional help with the information in this book.

For a free color catalog describing Gareth Stevens' list of high-quality books and multimedia programs, call 1-800-542-2595 (USA) or 1-800-461-9120 (Canada). Gareth Stevens Publishing's Fax: (414) 332-3567.

Library of Congress Cataloging-in-Publication Data available upon request from publisher.
Fax: (414) 332-3567 for the attention of the Publishing Records Department.

ISBN 0-8368-2735-X

This edition first published in 2000 by
Gareth Stevens Publishing
A World Almanac Education Group Company
330 West Olive Street, Suite 100
Milwaukee, WI 53212 USA

Original © 1997 by Zoë Books Limited, Winchester, England.
Additional end matter © 2000 by Gareth Stevens, Inc.

Illustrations: Virginia Gray

Photographic acknowledgments

The publishers wish to acknowledge, with thanks, the following photographic sources:
Cover: Werner Forman Archive, top right /National Museum of Anthropology, Mexico City, top left /Pigorini Museum of Prehistory and Ethnography, Rome, center /British Museum, London, bottom left and right.

Biblioteca Medicea Laurenziana, Florence 6, 7t, 9, 16t, 17t, 19b; The Bodleian Library, Oxford 8t (Ms. Arch. Selden A.1, fol.60r), 8b (Ms. Arch. Selden A.1, fol.68r), 13t (Ms. Arch. Selden A.1, fol.70r), 16b (Ms. Arch. Selden A.1, fol.61r), 18t, 20b (Ms. Arch. Selden A.1, fol.46r), 24t (Ms. Arch. Selden A.1, fol.63r); C. M. Dixon 10b, 14b; e. t. archive 15, 21t & b, 23b; Werner Forman Archive 10t, 11b /British Museum, London 3, 11t, 13b, 14t, 17b, 22b, 23t, 24b, 25t & c /Liverpool Museum, Liverpool 5b, 25b /Museum of the American Indian, New York 18b /Museum für Völkerkunde, Vienna, title page, 12b, 19t /National Museum of Anthropology, Mexico City 5t, 7b, 20t, 22t /Pigorini Museum of Prehistory and Ethnography, Rome 4b, 12t.

Printed in the United States of America

1 2 3 4 5 6 7 8 9 04 03 02 01 00

CONTENTS

Words that appear in the glossary are printed in
boldface type the first time they occur in the text.

INTRODUCTION

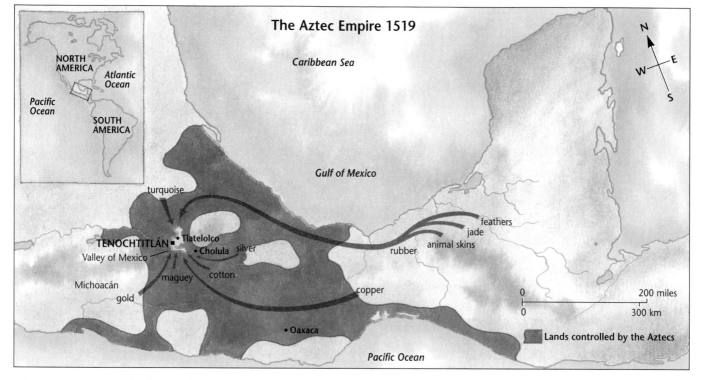

The Aztec Empire 1519

NORTH AMERICA
Atlantic Ocean
Pacific Ocean
SOUTH AMERICA

Caribbean Sea

Gulf of Mexico

turquoise

feathers
jade
animal skins

TENOCHTITLÁN • Tlatelolco
• Cholula   silver
Valley of Mexico   rubber

maguey   cotton

Michoacán
gold   copper

• Oaxaca

Pacific Ocean

0   200 miles
0   300 km

Lands controlled by the Aztecs

The Aztecs settled in what is now central Mexico more than 700 years ago. Other **Mesoamerican** peoples had already settled on the fertile farmland in the Valley of Mexico. These peoples were skilled in **crafts** such as stoneworking, pottery, basket making, weaving, textiles, and featherworking.

Names for the peoples

● The name *Aztec* comes from the word Aztlán. In Aztec **legend**, Aztlán was the homeland of the Mexica people. The Mexica left Aztlán and moved south to settle in the Valley of Mexico.
● Later, historians used the word *Aztec* to describe all the peoples who lived in the Valley of Mexico at the time of the Spanish **conquest**, nearly 500 years ago.

▲ This wooden mask is inlaid with turquoise and shells. It represents *Chalchiuhtlicue*, the goddess of water, rivers, and lakes.

▲ By the early 1500s, when Spanish explorers reached the coast of Central America, the Aztecs had built up a large **empire**. When Moctezuma II became the ruler, or *tlatoani*, in 1502, the empire was still growing. The Aztecs controlled lands that stretched from the Atlantic to the Pacific coasts.

The *tlatoani* ruled the Aztec empire from Tenochtitlán, the capital city. By 1500, more than a million people lived in the Valley of Mexico. About 250,000 of them lived in the city of Tenochtitlán.

The Mexica, as the Aztecs called themselves, were forced to settle on islands and swamplands in the lakes. However, they soon became the most powerful of all the valley peoples. From their island cities of Tenochtitlán and Tlatelolco, the Aztecs took control of the farmlands in the Valley of Mexico. The peoples living there also became known as the Mexica. Their craft skills became part of the Aztec tradition.

The Aztecs traded with peoples in different areas for the raw materials and goods that they needed or valued. The Tarascan peoples of Michoacán were skilled metalworkers. The Aztecs traded with them for copper bells, tweezers, needles, and axes.

Mixtec craft workers from Oaxaca made beautiful jewelry. They used gold and precious stones such as turquoise and jade, which were highly valued by the Aztecs.

▶ This Mixtec earring is made of gold. Tiny bells hang below the gold skull.

Laws and punishments

● The Aztecs had strict laws to control the peoples that they ruled. There were harsh punishments, including death, for those who disobeyed them.
● The laws covered every aspect of life, including the work people were allowed to do, the clothes they wore, and even the food they could eat.

By 1500 there were about 15 million people living in Aztec lands, both in the countryside and in the many towns and **city-states**. The Aztecs forced these people to pay **tribute** to them.

Goods such as woven mats, canoes, paper, feather cloaks, gold and jade jewelry, and raw materials such as rubber and animal skins, as well as corn (maize) and other foodstuffs, were all sent as tribute to Tenochtitlán.

◀ The Aztecs used picture symbols, or **glyphs**, rather than letters of the alphabet. They wrote on paper strips, which they folded like an accordian to make up a book, or codex. Much of the information about the Aztecs comes from the codices they made after the Spanish conquest. Spanish priests traveled all over the Aztec empire. Aztec **scribes** made records for them.

AZTEC CRAFTS

Reeds and clay

People living in the countryside made use of all the materials around them. In the Valley of Mexico, people gathered reeds from the marshes and lake shores to weave into baskets, mats, and furniture. They also used reeds to make **thatched** roofs for their houses.

They gathered the mud from the rivers and lakes to build house walls. They used clay, which they **molded** by hand and then baked hard in the sun, to make cooking utensils and pottery containers for storing food.

Wood

The Aztecs shaped wood into tools, such as digging sticks, to work the land and plant the crops. Their boats were wooden canoes made from hollowed-out tree trunks. The canoes carried goods, materials, and people around the lakes.

Farming and canals

● The Aztecs farmed in the Valley of Mexico. They dug out water channels, or canals, through the marshes around the lakes.
● Then they made small platforms of land called *chinampas* from the mud they had dug up.

◄ This codex drawing shows that there was little furniture inside an Aztec house. Most activities, such as cooking and sleeping, took place on or near the floor. The woven reed mat, or *petlatl*, was the most important item in the room. Small tables and stools were also made of woven reeds.

The Aztecs made finely woven baskets. They used them to store food and as containers for jewelry and other valuables. Square or rectangular baskets with lids were used to store clothes.

Baked clay, or **earthenware**, pots and pans of many shapes and sizes were used for cooking over an open fire.

◀ This farmer is using a wooden digging stick to make holes for the corn seeds he is planting. He has knotted his cloak to make a bag to carry the corn seeds. He has slung the bag around his neck, leaving both his hands free for working the land.

The drawing is from a codex made soon after the Spanish conquest.

The Aztecs built huge, pyramid-shaped stone platforms throughout the empire. These were temples to the gods. The temples were centers of learning. The priests studied **astronomy**, watching the stars and planets in the night sky. They produced an accurate yearly calendar, which they used to set and record dates for festivals. The priests were also **astrologers**. They foretold, or predicted, the best times for important events, such as planting or harvesting the crops.

The Aztecs had no other form of transport. They carried goods on their backs when they were traveling over land.

Stone

Stone was cut, or quarried, from the mountains that surrounded the Valley of Mexico. Important buildings, such as the ruler's palace in Tenochtitlán, were built with stone. It was also used to make sculptures of important gods or goddesses.

▼ This massive carved "stone of the five suns" once stood on the platform of the great pyramid at Tenochtitlán. The face of the sun god is carved in the center of the stone. Around it are four carvings of other sun gods. The broad band around these gods is carved with the Aztec signs for the names of the days in each month. The Aztecs divided their year into 18 months. Each month lasted 20 days.

The power of gods and goddesses
● The Aztecs feared the power of the gods and goddesses even more than the harsh laws made by their rulers. They believed that the gods and goddesses controlled everything about life. In their everyday life and their **religious** festivals, the Aztecs tried to please the gods and goddesses.

◀ All Aztec women, rich and poor, were expected to be skilled at weaving cloth. Mothers taught their daughters to spin thread and then to weave it into cloth. They used a simple backstrap loom, like the one shown in this codex drawing.

Cloth

The Aztecs made coarse cloth from the threads, or **fibers**, of the maguey cactus. Most people wore clothes made from maguey cloth. The thread was also strong enough to make bags, sandals, and fishing nets. Even the spines from the cactus plants were used as sewing needles.

▲ A woman is spinning thread on a spindle.

Children at work

● All Aztec children had to help in the household. Boys had to carry water and firewood. Girls had to clean the house and prepare food.
● Parents were expected to pass on their skills to their children. While young girls learned to cook and to weave, young boys learned to hunt and to fish.

The Aztecs planted the maguey cactus in highland areas where the land was poor. The climate was too dry or cold there for food crops to grow well. They also planted the nopal cactus and gathered the insects that fed on this plant. They used them to make cochineal, a reddish pink dye used for coloring inks and dyeing clothes.

Cotton was grown in the warmer lowland areas and was spun into fine cloth. Aztec laws allowed only nobles from the ruling class, or *pipiltin*, to wear cotton clothes.

Paper and glue

● People collected the bark from the wild fig tree to make paper. They soaked it and then beat it into sheets. Then they coated it with a chalky varnish. The sheets were stuck together in long strips. The glue was often made from droppings, or bat dung, which they collected from the countryside.

● The paper strips, which could be up to 36 feet (11 m) long, were folded like an accordion. Scribes drew on both sides of the paper.

Markets and towns

Most people who lived in the countryside had the skills to make most of the things they needed for everyday life. However, people who lived in the towns depended upon farmers and traders to bring them the food, raw materials, and other goods they needed. Town markets were held every day.

The free men and women who worked the land or had a trade or craft were called *macehualtin*. Every Aztec town was divided into neighborhoods. These were controlled by different groups, or *calpulli*.

People who werc born into a *calpulli* were often skilled craft workers, such as cloth dyers, jewelers, potters, scribes, or stone or metal workers, who made tools or weapons. These *macehualtin* worked from their own homes and passed on their skills to their children.

At the market

● The Aztec markets were well laid out, with different goods sold in different areas. The market officials fixed the prices. The Aztecs did not use coins to buy goods. They used cacao beans instead. Sometimes people exchanged, or **bartered**, using other goods such as paper or tools.

◀ This farmer and his wife are storing seeds of the amaranth plant in containers.
The two smaller storage jars are made of clay. The larger container may have been made from strips of straw or reeds.

Pottery

The Aztecs used clay to make many different objects, from toys to musical instruments. They shaped and decorated the clay by hand.

▲ Clay models of Aztec household gods and goddesses

The Aztecs loved flowers, particularly dahlias, which farmers grew alongside their food crops. Even the poorest households had a clay vase for flowers. They also had small clay models of the gods and goddesses who were important for the household.

Household gods and goddesses

● Each family chose its household gods and goddesses, who looked after every part of life.
● There were gods and goddesses for different types of craft work. Xochiquetzal was the goddess of flowers, painters, and weavers.
● Huitzilopochtli was one of the most important Aztec gods. He was the god associated with the sun and war.
● There were different Aztec gods or goddesses for each day and night of the year. Some of these may have been chosen because members of the family were born on a particular day or night.

◀ A pottery rattle, showing a woman holding a child

The finest Aztec pottery came from Cholula. It was made from earthenware of many colors. The clay was shaped and worked until it was very thin. Then it was left to harden. The colors used to decorate the pottery were made from rocks and **minerals**. The fine designs were similar to those painted and drawn by the Aztec scribes.

Cholula pottery was used in the *tlatoani's* palace. Only the *pipiltin* and the priests were allowed to use this highly decorated pottery. The *macehualtin* used earthenware dishes that had no fine decoration.

◀ Aztec potters also made dishes like this one. They were used by priests in special ceremonies at the temples.

The use of the wheel

● Although the Aztecs made simple wheels for use on pull-along toys, they did not use wheels in other practical ways. People carried goods on their backs overland, rather than using carts with wheels. Important people were carried around on **litters**.

● The Spanish conquerors introduced the potter's wheel, for making pots, dishes, and other rounded objects. Before this, the Aztecs made even the most perfectly rounded plates and bowls by hand.

▼ Decorated Aztec pottery dishes

Gold and feathers

Many craft workers lived in Tenochtitlán. There the most precious and expensive craft goods were bought by the *pipiltin* and the rich merchants. The most highly valued craft goods were made out of gold, precious stones, and feathers.

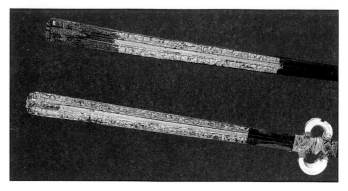

▲ The Aztecs used spears as weapons and for hunting. They had wooden spear throwers, called *atlatl*, which were used to give the spears extra thrust. Some spear throwers, like the one shown here, were carved and then covered with gold.

Rich merchants

● Some of the raw materials for the crafts came from lands that were not controlled by the Aztecs, around the southern Gulf of Mexico. Merchants, called *pochteca*, traveled great distances to trade for goods such as jade and turquoise, rubber, animal skins, and the brightly colored feathers from **tropical** birds.

● Although the *pochteca* were rich, they were not allowed to show their wealth outside their own homes. When they went out, they wore simple clothes made of maguey cloth, like the *macehualtin*.

The whole family worked together to make objects, such as shields, from feathers. The children made the glue from bat dung. The women sorted and dyed the feathers. The men drew the design for the object onto a piece of cloth. They cut the dyed feathers into shapes and attached them to the cloth. Then the cloth was glued onto a backing board. When this

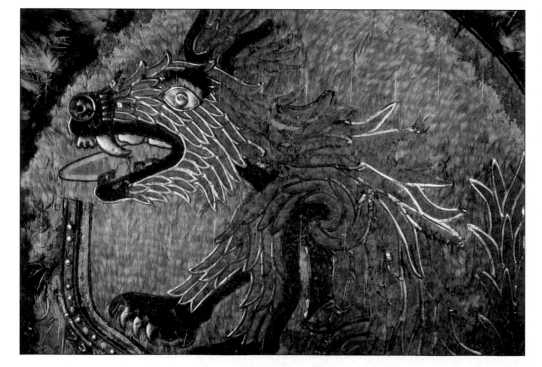

◄ This featherwork shield may have been owned by the *tlatoani*. The eyes, teeth, claws, and fur of the animal are made out of thin strips of gold. The turquoise feathers probably came from the humming bird.

▲ Featherworkers make a headdress for a noble customer.

The goldsmiths' work

● Sometimes goldsmiths wove thin strips of silver and gold together, so that they looked like lace. This was called filigree work.

● They used a model or cast, made of clay, to make some gold objects. When the clay model was dry, they covered it with beeswax. Then they coated it with more clay. The model was heated until the wax ran out through a hole in the bottom of the cast. Hot, liquid, or molten, gold was poured in and allowed to cool. Then the clay cast was broken, and the gold object taken out. This way of casting gold was called the "lost-wax" method.

● Sometimes goldsmiths used both casting and filigree methods to make a gold object.

was dry, the final layer of feathers was attached, and the pattern was outlined with thin strips of gold. Mixtec goldsmiths worked from Tenochtitlán. They made the gold jewelry and ornaments bought by the *pipiltin*. They used materials such as silver, turquoise, and jade with the gold.

◄ Quetzalcoatl, the "feathered serpent," was the god of the winds. He was shown in many different forms.
  This Aztec sculpture is made of jade.

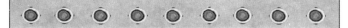

◀ This obsidian mirror is called a "smoking mirror." It was used by Aztec priests. They would gaze into the mirror and see clouds of smoke. Then the smoke would part, and they would see a **vision**.

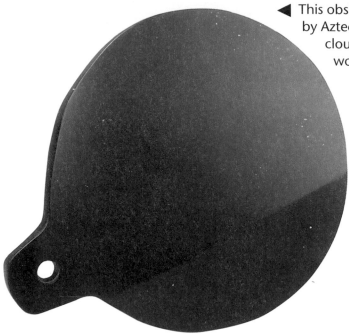

Stone for tools and weapons

● A hard, black, glassy, volcanic rock called obsidian was used to make sharp-edged tools for splitting and carving stone and for weapons. This natural shiny glass was also used to make masks, mirrors, and jewelry.

Stonework

Stoneworking was one of the oldest of all the Mesoamerican crafts, and one of the most important. Huge stone blocks were used to build temples and palaces, and for sculptures.

Great skill was needed to split stone such as obsidian and flint, to make cutting blades for knives and other tools. Many craft workers, including those who made **mosaic** decorations, needed sharp blades.

The ballgame of *tlachtli* was played on a long stone court, close to a temple. The court was shaped like the letter I.

Stone rings were attached high up on the walls at the center of the court. Players tried to hit a solid rubber ball through one of the stone rings, using only their hips or their knees.

The players were specially trained and wore gloves, belts, and padded hipguards to protect themselves. Only the *pipiltin* could play, but everyone could go and watch. *Tlachtli* was played on important festival days.

▲ This Aztec dagger has a blade made of flint and a handle decorated with turquoise mosaic. It was used only by the Eagle warriors, for **human sacrifice**.

The winner at *tlachtli* was surrounded by the crowd who had been watching the game. They sang songs and danced with the winner. He was given a special prize of a feather cloak. However, the greatest prize for him was winning the game.

Games and gambling

The Aztecs liked to gamble. They placed bets on the teams that played *tlachtli*. Everyone, rich and poor, played a game like backgammon called *patolli*. Some gamblers even carried their *patolli* mats around with them.

The *patolli* mat was marked with 52 squares. The players threw beans, marked with white dots for numbers, as dice. Six red and blue pebbles were moved around the mat, according to the number that came up. Each player tried to get three pebbles in a row, to win the game.

Sometimes gamblers lost their homes, their jewelry, and even their clothes. The law was the same for the *pipiltin* and the *macehualtin*. If they could not pay their gambling debts, they could be forced to sell themselves as slaves.

▲ This codex drawing shows people praying to Macuilxochitl, "five flowers," the god of flowers, song, dance, and games. They are about to play *patolli*.

CLOTHES AND JEWELRY

Clothes laws

Most Aztec clothes were simply made. They were not shaped to fit closely. Aztec laws were strict about the type and length of material used. Only the *pipiltin* were allowed to wear long clothes made of cotton. The *macehualtin* had to wear clothes made from maguey fiber that ended at the knee.

However, there was little difference in the styles of clothing worn by the *pipiltin* and the *macehualtin*. All men wore loin cloths, which covered the area from their waists to their thighs. Women wore lengths of cloth that were sewn or knotted to make blouses and skirts.

▲ This gardener is using his cloak to carry the plants he has gathered. All *macehualtin* went barefoot. Only the *pipiltin* were allowed to wear sandals.

The skirt was sometimes held around the waist with a belt.

◄ This codex drawing shows two young people getting married. Their clothes are knotted together, which made them husband and wife.

▲ The two merchants in this codex drawing are wearing plain cloaks, knotted over the right shoulder. The warrior on the right wears a decorated cloak and a feather headdress. The merchants' goods include cloaks, jewelry, and cutting blades.

The cape or cloak was the most important garment worn by men. The plain, undyed cloak worn by many *macehualtin* was a rectangular blanket, knotted at the neck. The people used the same cloak as a blanket at night.

The material used for a cloak, and the type of decorations on it, showed the importance of the person wearing it. Some *pipiltin* had cotton cloaks edged with precious jewels or embroidered with gold thread. Sometimes rabbit fur was woven into the cotton cloth,

to make a warm winter cloak. The very best cloaks were made out of brightly colored feathers.

Warriors who were brave in battle were given cloaks or jewelry as a reward. The decorations on their cloaks and the jewelry they wore showed others how brave and how successful they were.

The Aztec laws controlled people's appearance from head to toe. The punishment for disobeying these laws was death.

Hairstyles

Warriors tied up their hair into topknots. The bravest and most successful warriors wore the most elaborate topknots, often held in place with decorated bands of cloth. Working men, such as farmers, wore their hair loose, in a simpler style.

Aztec women wore their hair long. Unmarried women wore their hair loose, while married women plaited their hair. They wound the plaits around their heads, so that the ends stuck out at each side. The plaits were held in place with bands of cloth. If the woman came from a *pipiltin* family, her hairband might be decorated with jewels.

▶ Aztec warriors and women painted patterns on their faces for special occasions, such as weddings or festivals. The Aztecs liked bright colors. Girls often used yellow or red dyes on their faces. They used clay stamps like these to print the patterns on their skin.

Keeping clean

The Aztecs washed their faces with clean water. Aztec men did not shave. They used tweezers to remove unwanted hair from their faces. Parents taught their children to wash their hands before they ate. Clothes were washed regularly. It was important for Aztec families to be clean and neat.

Taking a steam bath

● Most Aztec families had a mud bathhouse in the yard. They lit a fire outside, against the back wall of the bathhouse. When the wall was hot, they went inside and threw water against the wall to make steam. Then they beat themselves with bundles of twigs to clean their skin.

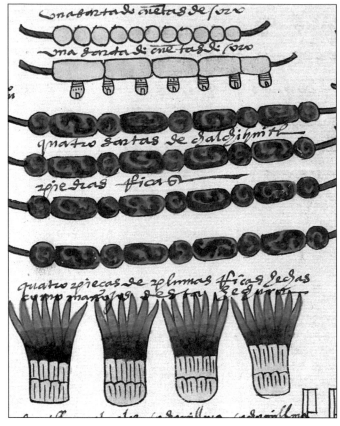

▲ This codex page shows part of an Aztec tribute list. The drawings show jade and gold necklaces and bunches of green feathers.

Jewelry

Most people had pierced ears and wore ear plugs of shell or polished stones. Only the *pipiltin* could wear jewelry such as lip and nose plugs made from precious stones or gold.

The *tlatoani* wore gold armbands, anklets, and gold rattles on his feet. A few of the *pipiltin* who advised him were also allowed to wear this type of jewelry.

▲ Aztec gold lip plugs

Moctezuma II

This description of the last Aztec ruler was written by the conquistador Bernal Diaz at the time of the Spanish conquest.

"... The great Moctezuma was about forty years old, of good height, well proportioned, spare, and slight. He did not wear his hair long but just over his ears, and he had a short black beard, well-shaped and thin. He was very neat and clean, and took a bath every afternoon. The clothes he wore one day he did not wear again till three or four days later.

"When they [the nobles] entered his room, they had to take off their rich cloaks and put on poor-looking cloaks. They had to be clean and walk barefoot, with their eyes downcast, for they were not allowed to look him in the face. As they approached him, they bowed low three times, saying 'Lord, my lord, my great lord'...."

▲ Moctezuma II sent this headdress as a gift for the King of Spain. It is made of the materials that the Aztecs most valued — gold, precious stones and turquoise, and green feathers from tropical birds.

The green feathers from the quetzal bird were the most precious of all. This bird was linked with the Aztec god Quetzalcoatl.

◄ In this codex drawing, the *tlatoani* is sitting on the left, wearing a turquoise headdress and cloak. The nobles are wearing simple cloaks, without rich decorations.

Clothes for war

The *tlatoani* was the ruler of the Aztec empire and the commander of the army. The people expected him to wage war as often as possible, so that the Aztecs could gain land and tribute from the people they defeated.

The army

● The successful warrior units led the army into battle. Sometimes there were as many as 200,000 soldiers.

● The warriors came from every *capulli*. In Tenochtitlán, for example, each *capulli* had to send 400 men to fight. Each unit was commanded by a leader from its own *capulli*.

▼ This detail from a codex page shows the headgear, warsuit, shields, and items of jewelry worn by the Eagle warriors.

▲ This piece of Aztec gold and turquoise jewelry was worn on the chest. Its design is similar to that drawn on the codex page. An Eagle warrior may have worn it.

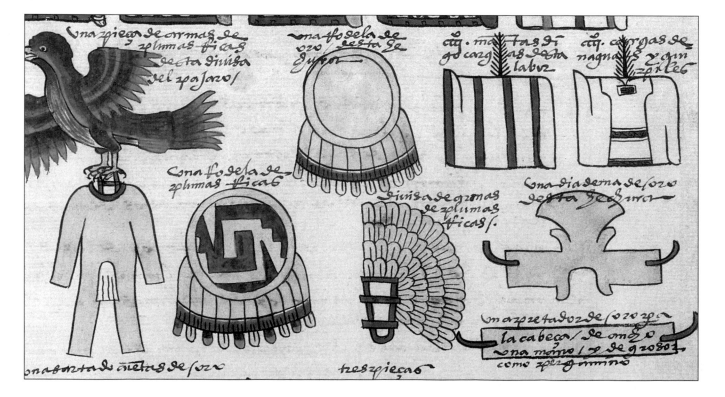

▲ These warriors are dressed in different animal skins. They hold swords set with sharp stone blades and carry highly decorated shields. One warrior has an elaborate feather headdress.

The *tlatoani* was advised by the most experienced and successful Aztec warriors. The best soldiers were grouped into units, such as the Eagle and Jaguar warriors. They wore headgear, jewelry, and cloaks that showed which unit they were part of.

There were ceremonies for successful warriors who joined these units. They were given special warsuits. The *pipiltin* wore feather warsuits, while the suits of the *macehualtin* were made of animal skins.

The *tlatoani* rewarded brave warriors by giving them land, weapons, clothes, and jewelry.

▼ The *tlatoani* presents a feather headdress to a warrior.

A great store of weapons and armor

Bernal Diaz describes the store kept by Moctezuma at his palace in Tenochtitlán.

"... Moctezuma had two houses stocked with every sort of weapon. Many of them were richly adorned with gold and precious stones. There were shields large and small, and two-handed swords set with flint blades that cut much better than our swords .... In fact they cut like razors, and the Indians [Aztecs] can shave their heads with them .... There was also a great deal of cotton armor, richly worked on the outside with different colored feathers, which they used as distinguishing marks, and they had helmets made of wood and bone, which were also highly decorated with feathers on the outside ...."

FESTIVALS

Music, dancing, and poetry

The Aztecs believed that their lives were in the hands of the gods and goddesses. The people loved singing, dancing, music, and poetry, but they were always afraid of death.

An Aztec poem

Does one really live upon the earth?
Not forever on the earth, only for a short time
 here
Even jade shatters
Even gold breaks
Even quetzal plumes tear
Not forever on the earth, only a short time here.

Aztec children went to a special school called a *telpochcalli*, a "youth house." Each *calpulli* had such a school, attached to the local temple. The priests taught the boys and girls separately. They learned about their history and religion, and they learned how to **recite** stories and poetry.

▲ Xochipilli, "the flower prince," is shown here singing and accompanying himself with a rattle in each hand. The rattles are now missing from the sculpture.

◄ Dancers used these small pottery whistles to mark time while they danced at festivals.

◀ This two-tone drum was played to give rhythm for the dancers. The outside is made of carved wood. The top of the drum had two pieces of wood, which produced different tones when the drummer hit them.

Older children went to the *cuiciacalli*, the "house of song," where priests taught them to play musical instruments and to sing. They also learned the special songs and dances of the different festivals.

There was a festival for every one of the 18 months in the Aztec year. Each festival was in honor of a different group of gods or goddesses. Many festivals were linked to the seasons and the patterns of farming.

Tecuilhuitontli, "the small feast of the lords," was held during month 7 (June) of the Aztec year. By this time the rainy season had begun. Plants and crops were beginning to grow well. Xochipilli, the god of flowers, plants, song, and dance, was honored at this time.

There was much music and dancing during this festival. Dancers sometimes dressed in colorful costumes to represent the gods and goddesses.

Many noble households kept their own orchestra and entertainers to play for their guests. The *tlatoani* danced and gave gifts to the people at *Tecuilhuitontli*, and the *pipiltin* held feasts for the *macehualtin*.

▶ This codex drawing shows men shaking rattles made from **gourds**, and drummers playing two different types of drums.

Priests and temples

Priests at the temples held ceremonies every day. They beat great drums or blew on trumpets made from conch shells.

Burning incense

● Priests burned **incense** as an offering to the gods. They did this four times during the day and five times at night. The Spanish priest Bernardino de Sahagún described this, just after the Spanish conquest.

"The first time ... as it became dark. The second time when we were going to sleep. The third time was when they sounded the trumpets made of shells. The fourth time was at midnight. And the fifth time was just before dawn...."

▲ This codex drawing shows one priest burning incense and another playing a drum.

The temples were full of the sound of music at every festival. Singers and dancers were accompanied by flutes, drums, rattles, copper bells, and clay whistles.

At some festivals the priests led processions out into the countryside to special places, or **shrines**. *Tepeilhuitl*, the "feast of the mountains," was held during month 8 (October). People took offerings to the shrines on important mountains for the rain god, Tlaloc, and for other gods and goddesses.

Matmakers, fishermen, weavers, embroiderers, and painters all made special offerings at this festival. These were models of the gods and goddesses, fashioned from dough which they made from amaranth flour.

▲ Aztec priests often burned *copal*, an incense made from the **resin** of pine trees. They used containers called incense burners. This decorated clay incense burner has a handle shaped like a turkey claw.

The *tlatoani* was the chief of all the priests, as well as the ruler of the Aztec empire. He led the ceremonies for Tlaloc during the feast of the mountains. He also took part in all the main festivals during the Aztec year.

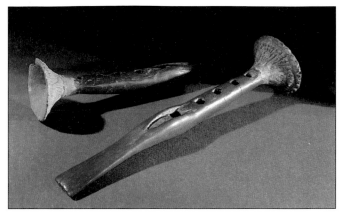

▲ Two small Aztec flutes

▲ This wind instrument is called an ocarina. It is made out of clay, shaped in the form of a turtle.

► This drawing of the *tlatoani* has been made in the Mixtec style. It shows the ruler sitting on his throne, wearing an elaborate feather headdress and a highly decorated cloak. He is also wearing a nose plug made of precious stones.

Dressing the Aztec way

The Aztecs dressed up for festivals every month of the year. Sometimes they walked in a procession to a shrine on a hilltop, or by a river or lake. They also dressed up to go to watch the ballgame, *tlachtli*, and for special family occasions, such as the birth of a child or a marriage.

All Aztec people had a bath before they dressed for a special occasion.

Here are some suggestions for ways you could dress and prepare for a special event or festival in the Aztec way.

Remember that only people from noble Aztec families, the *pipiltin*, could wear long clothes and sandals. Other Aztecs, such as the *macehualtin*, wore clothes that ended at the knee and went barefoot.

You will need: • one plain white sheet or a large tablecloth • a smaller tablecloth or small towel, for a belt or loin cloth.

To make a cloak:

1. Knot the sheet around your neck.

2. Knot the smaller piece of material around your waist, under the cloak, to make a loin cloth.

3. Adjust the length of the cloak by changing the position of the knot around your neck.

To make a dress:

1. Knot the sheet around your neck.

2. Loosely tie the smaller piece of material around your waist over the sheet to make a belt.

3. Adjust the length of the dress by pulling up the material under the belt.

4. When the dress is the right length, tighten the belt around your waist. The belt will hold the dress in position.

The Aztecs decorated their clothes with patterns. They liked to use bright colors. Make a pattern for your cloak or dress. You could copy one of these Aztec designs, or make up one of your own.

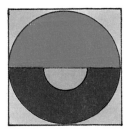 

You could make one big patterned square to decorate your clothes, or you could make several smaller patterns. Choose your favorite colors for the pattern.

You will need: ● a large, square sheet of white paper ● scissors ● a pencil ● a set of colored pens or pencils ● safety pins ● transparent sealing tape.

1. If you are making several patterns, fold the sheet of paper into small squares.

2. Draw your pattern in pencil onto the paper. Color it in. Make sure you have color in every square, if you are making several patterns.

3. Cut out your design or your patterns in strips or squares.

4. Lay out your cloak or dress flat on the floor or a table. Place your design or patterned squares on the material and fix them in position with safety pins.

5. Try the clothes on to make sure your designs are in the right place.

6. Carefully take off the clothes. Use sealing tape to fix your patterns onto the material. Take out the safety pins. Your cloak or dress is now ready to wear, for a special occasion or festival.

Paint your face like an Aztec

Priests covered their skin with black paint. Aztec warriors also used black paint to draw a thick black line across their faces, from ear to ear. On special occasions, most Aztecs decorated their faces with brightly patterned designs. They used pottery face stamps to do this.

Here are some of the designs the Aztecs used for pottery face stamps.

Choose a design to paint on your face. Remember that the Aztecs liked to use bright colors, such as red or yellow.

You will need: ● a set of face paints ● a mirror ● a washcloth.

1. Choose the design you like best. Practice drawing it on the back of your hand, using a stick of face paint.

2. When you are happy with the design on your hand, look at it in a mirror. You will see that the design is reversed on the mirror image.

3. Choose a bright face paint color that suits you. Use it to copy the design on your hand onto each cheek. If you go wrong, wipe off the design with a damp washcloth and start again.

4. You could also decorate your arms and the back of your hands with face paints. You could use different designs or colors to do this.

Hair and headbands

Remember that some Aztec men and young women used cloth headbands to hold their hair in position. If they were nobles or warriors, the headbands were highly colored or decorated with gold and precious jewels.

Young, unmarried women wore their hair loose. Married women plaited their hair and wound it around their heads. Warriors wore their hair in topknots.

Choose an Aztec hairstyle and make a headband to hold it in position.

You will need: ● a big white handkerchief or a white cloth table napkin ● a pack of colored paper stickers, of different shapes and sizes.

1. Lay the cloth flat on the table and then fold it like this.

2. Make sure that the headband is big enough to tie around your head, with a knot at the back.

3. Stick the colored squares onto the front of the headband to make a pattern.

Aztec performers

Once the Aztecs had bathed, dressed, made up, and done their hair, they were ready to perform at a special occasion or a festival. The Aztecs danced to the rhythm of whistles, bells, and drums. They often danced in a circle around the musicians. Aztec musicians played wind instruments, such as the flute, and sang songs. On special occasions, everyone recited poems or stories they had learned.

You and your friends could put on a show. Here are some suggestions for the things that you could do.

1. Choose a poem or short story that you like, or make one up. Learn it by heart and practice saying it out loud.

2. Choose a song you like to sing, or a piece of music that you can whistle or play on a wind instrument. Your friends could make up a rhythm to accompany it, using shakers and rattles or drums.

3. Make up a rhythm for a dance. Then practice dancing to it, in a big circle around the musicians.

GLOSSARY

astrologer: Someone who studies the effects that the movements of the stars and planets may have on people's actions and behavior on Earth.

astronomy: The scientific study of the stars and planets and other objects in space.

barter: To use goods to buy other goods, instead of using money. If the goods were different in price or value, the Aztecs often used cacao beans to make up the difference.

city-state: A small state or area of land, which is centered on a single city and governed by it.

conquest: The victory of one country or people over another, usually through battles or wars. The Spanish not only defeated the Aztecs in A.D. 1521 but also took control of their lands and ruled the Aztec empire as a Spanish colony, or part of Spain.

craft: Any trade or pastime in which people use skill to make things by hand.

earthenware: Plain, unglazed pottery.

empire: A group of countries or states ruled by a single government or a single ruler or emperor.

fiber: A threadlike substance, often taken from plants or animals, used by the Aztecs mainly to weave cloth.

glyphs: Picture writing in which one symbol may stand for a word.

gourd: A large, fleshy fruit with a hard skin. The dried fruits with their seeds inside them were often used as musical instruments by the Aztecs. They were shaken to give rhythm for the Aztec dancers.

human sacrifice: Killing a person to please the gods and goddesses. The Aztecs cut out people's hearts to offer to their gods.

incense: A material burned to give off a sweet-smelling fragrance, which is often used during religious ceremonies.

legend: An old story that many people believe, even though it may not be quite true.

litter: A seat or bed slung between two poles, which was carried on the shoulders by a team of men. Some litters had a cover, or canopy, to protect the person being carried from the sun or rain.

Mesoamerican: Describes peoples who lived in central and southern Mexico, Guatemala, and parts of El Salvador and Honduras. It was in these areas that civilizations flourished between 1000 B.C. and A.D. 1521.

minerals: Useful substances that can be extracted from the earth, such as metals and gemstones.

molded: Made in a hollow form, which shapes materials such as clay, plaster, molten metals, or glass.

mosaic: A decoration or picture made from tiny chips of colored stone or glass. The Aztecs used precious stones to make mosaic masks.

recite: To repeat something from memory, such as a poem or a story. Aztec children were trained to do this for an audience. Aztec men and women were expected to be able to speak well in public.

religious: Concerned with religion and the gods and goddesses.

resin: The sap that oozes from a pine tree, forming a sticky gum.

scribe: Someone whose job is to write things out by hand, or to keep written records.

shrine: A place or building linked with a god or a holy person. People often leave offerings, such as food or flowers, at a shrine.

thatch: To make a roof of dried straw or reeds.

tribute: Regular payments in goods or money made by one state or area to another. The Aztecs threatened and sometimes went to war with the states or areas that refused to pay tribute to them or that did not keep up their regular payments to the Aztecs.

tropical: From the middle and hottest part of the world, between the lines made by the Tropic of Cancer to the north and the Tropic of Capricorn to the south.

vision: A vivid idea or picture in the mind, sometimes to do with things that might happen in the future.

FURTHER READING

Aztec Times. If You Were There (series). Antony Mason and Andrea D. Pinkney, ed. (Simon & Schuster)

The Aztecs. The Ancient World (series). Robert Hull (Raintree/Steck-Vaughn)

The Aztecs. History Beneath Your Feet (series). Peter Crisp ((Raintree/Steck-Vaughn)

The Aztecs. Understanding People in the Past (series). Rosemary Rees (Heinemann)

Daily Life of the Aztecs. David Carrasco (Greenwood Publishing)

A Day with an Aztec. Pablo Escalante (Runestone)

Land of the Five Suns. Looking at Aztec Myths and Legends (series). Kay McManus (NTC Publishing)

Montezuma and the Fall of the Aztecs. Eric. A. Kimmel (Holiday House)

INDEX